The Blueprint to Affiliate Marketing

Revealed My Million Dollar Earning
Strategies, Tips, and Tricks

by Dan Moskel

Copyright © 2013 Dan Moskel
All Rights Reserved.

ISBN-13:
978-1494310943

ISBN-10:
1494310945

Table of Contents

Section 1 - The Basics......................6

Chapter 1 - What is Affiliate Marketing ... REALLY? 7

Chapter 2 - How EXACTLY ... Does It Work?...................................9

Chapter 3 - Is Affiliate Marketing a Scam? 11

Section 2 - The 7 Step Blueprint To Get Started 16

Chapter 4 - Choose Your Niche Market 17

Chapter 5 - Build a Website 20

Chapter 6 - Market Research ... Go To The MONEY 23

Chapter 7 - Getting Paid ... Affiliate Networks...28

Chapter 8 - Easiest Way to Get Started 40

Chapter 9 - Related Products and Services 45

Chapter 10 - Make Money Online ... NOW 48

Section 3 - The 7 Best, Proven, Ways To Drive Traffic To Your Website Including Quick, Easy, And Free Methods 50

Chapter 11 - The 7 Best & Proven Traffic Sources Overview................51

Chapter 12 - SEO, Search Engine Optimization, Free, Natural, Organic Search Traffic 57

Chapter 13 - Strategy ... Target Buying Keywords 63

Chapter 14 - Email Marketing 71

Chapter 15 - YouTube Videos 76

Chapter 16 - Pay-Per-Click Advertising 80

Chapter 17 - Content Network 84

Chapter 18 - Social Media ... and Other People 86

Chapter 19 - Take It Offline 90

Section 4 - Advanced Tips to Make Money with Affiliate Marketing 92

Chapter 20 - Copywriting Tips 93

Chapter 21 - Best Website Placement with Affiliate Marketing Banners 95

Section 1 - The Basics

Chapter 1 - What is Affiliate Marketing ... REALLY?

Affiliate marketing is exactly like a commission based sales position. Your job is to sell other businesses products and services, for them.

Did you know Walmart, Amazon, iTunes, and many more Fortune 500 companies provide you the ability to use affiliate marketing for their products and services?

Let me share one example of affiliate marketing in action, I recently received a postcard in the mail from Bluehost one of the biggest web hosting companies ... this company hosts all of my WordPress websites.

The postcard I received, was marketing the Google AdWords service, an online advertising platform, this is affiliate marketing in action.

The web hosting company Bluehost, is using their list of customers to help promote and build the Google AdWords online advertising business.

Affiliate marketing is legit. It is not some new creation that came along as a result of the internet. There have been businesses working with other businesses for many decades prior to the creation of the internet.

The reason you use this is to help serve your customers and clients better. In addition, you can create and generate more revenue for your business.

Chapter 2 - How EXACTLY ... Does It Work?

The short idea, is you are the sales force. Your job is the salesman. You will get paid based upon how many sales or leads you can create for another business.

There are a variety of ways to use affiliate marketing to earn money, however the amount of money you earn, will be based upon your performance.

One of the most common ways to use affiliate marketing is to place banners or advertisements on your website. To do this you will need to work with an affiliate marketing network or advertiser directly.

They will provide you a code, you can copy and paste into your website along with additional marketing materials that can include a toll free phone number, but more about all this later.

It is very smart to collect lead information from your website visitors too, as in their email address. This way you can continue to send helpful, useful, and relevant information to continue serving and marketing to your list. Follow up is key.

Chapter 3 - Is Affiliate Marketing a Scam?

During our research for this book, we were surprised to see many folks are searching if affiliate marketing is a scam?

Let me share two stories of real people that have used affiliate marketing and what it has provided their life.

Ben's story

Ben had dreams of living the Boston Legal TV show … sipping cognac and smoking cigars with William Shatner after winning big court cases.

But those dreams went up in smoke, shortly after graduating from law school, he was hit hard by the cubicle Dilbert reality of the real world: a 90min daily work commute, zoning out the first hour of every word day. And his new dream quickly shifted to just quitting his job and moving to a tropical island.

He didn't quit though, he persevered and after a few tough years working as a full-time cubicle Dilbert attorney he was ... in his words able to "retire" from practicing law.

This was all made possible using affiliate marketing. But, it doesn't take a law degree to be successful in this industry.

Dan's story

Dan was a college dropout working as a part time bartender ... he choose to drop out of school and started working with affiliate marketing.

It took a lot of time and work, but Dan was able to create an affluent income, go back to school and graduate while paying tuition, and continuing to run his online affiliate marketing business.

Dan is no genius. He lost the ability to communicate when he had a brain aneurism rupture at 12 years old.

He spent 6 weeks in the hospital, had his skull taken apart in surgery, and endured the humbling experience of consciously wetting the bed, due to his inability to communicate that he needed to pee.

In spite of all this, he slowly learned how to use use affiliate marketing and created a career for himself.

Yes, I am Dan and while it is true I've earned over a million dollars through affiliate marketing much of that income has been spent using online advertising methods including the earlier example of Google AdWords.

I've been working with affiliate marketing full time since 2006. It has been an incredible experience taking me all over the country, and really living a dream lifestyle.

It was instrumental in financing a TV commercial with DirecTV and providing me with the opportunity to appear on ESPN, MTV, VH-1, A&E, Comedy Central and many more national TV cable networks.

In this book, I want to reveal exactly how I got started, and how you can too, even if you have a shoestring budget.

I also want to share the 7 best traffic sources that I use including some free and quick methods, advanced techniques I've learned, and give you an easy to follow, step by step guide to get started with affiliate marketing.

I'm also going to show you, how I'm currently and continuing to use affiliate marketing to help grow all three of my online businesses and how you can do the same for your business.

Let's be honest

Listen, affiliate marketing is not a get rich quick scheme, it does have the ability to make you rich quick, just like any business venture ... but it's rarely going to happen overnight.

You must be willing to put in the work, time, and investment first.

Avoid being like the man, the great Earl Nightingale speaks of:

"Who sat in front of the stove and said give me heat, and then I'll put in the wood."

You must put in the wood first, before you can receive the heat.

I'm here to help YOU and want to give you a short cut simple system to get you started and maximize your earnings with affiliate marketing. Many of these advanced tips I encourage you to review again, and again once you have some proven revenue being earned.

How to get maximum value from this book

I strongly advise you to simply "barrow" many of my strategies. And, visit DanMoskelUniversity.com to sign up for your free bonus affiliate marketing training videos.

This is a legit method of earning money online.

But, like everything it does require an investment of your time, work, and talent.

Along with the blueprint to how a total beginner can get started earning money with affiliate marketing ... this is what I will tell my sweet 3 year old nephew, my cousins, friends, family, loved ones, and the most important person ... YOU!

Section 2 - The 7 Step Blueprint To Get Started

Chapter 4 - Choose Your Niche Market

The very first step is to choose your niche market. This is what you will write and create your website about, along with developing your marketing materials around.

It is key to follow your interests, passions, desires, and current knowledge. Harvest the acres of diamonds, you already posses.

If you do this, it will be monumental in how effective you can market yourself and your business. And the best part is, it will make your work, feel like play.

- What is your current job?

- What do you know about?

- What have you experienced lately?

Maybe your a great cook like our friend Alex. Or a tech savvy individual like our pal James, or maybe your passion is like our friend Claire working to increase awareness for a good cause. And my sweet 3 year old nephew, I'm sure could tell me about all the coolest kids toys.

Whatever it is that your interested in or experienced with, is an EXCELLENT topic for you to work around.

You can and will always be expanding and building your business, in order to reach additional markets. But, initially I would suggest that you create information about what you already know. And get busy harvesting the acres of diamonds, you currently have.

Ben the "retired" attorney had less than perfect credit, he had to first fix his credit, before he could become a licensed practicing attorney. This is subject that got Ben started with affiliate marketing. On a side, the sub prime credit industry is a massive market.

When I was 20 years old, I had the dream of helping guys like my roommate talk to women, and date women.

I slowly turned this dream into a reality, and actually ran a national TV commercial with DirecTV, using online advertising.

I got started within the sub prime credit niche because I started working with Ben. But, as time passed I started also working with men's dating advice, and today I'm sharing with you, what is the most valuable that I have ... my online affiliate marketing knowledge.

Follow what you already have knowledge about, and are interested in. This doesn't mean you can't work in additional even unrelated markets, but this is the best place to get started.

Chapter 5 - Build a Website

The second step is building your website. This is not the only way to earn money with affiliate marketing, but I definitely recommend it.

If you don't have a budget or are working on a shoestring budget, I would suggest that you minimize your initial investment and avoid purchasing web hosting which is about $100 annually.

Instead, you can use Blogger, a company owned by Google, as your content management system, and purchase a custom domain name for less than $12 per year. This is what I have used for DanMoskelUniversity.com.

As your business grows, and you earn enough money to justify investing $100 every year with your website, then we would suggest purchasing web hosting and paying for a professional design. But not until your earning a substantial income from your business.

Your third option, is to build a free website using Blogger or WordPress. However, if you pursue this option your website domain or address will appears as:

websitedoman.blogspot.com

or

websitedomain.wordpress.com

Caution

Years ago I had a WordPress website that was not on a custom domain erased because I believe I violated their terms of service, by using affiliate marketing links.

It is smart in my opinion, to spend a minimum investment of $12 and get a custom domain name. We use GoDaddy for ours.

You can of course, go all out and buy web-hosing and a professional website design. We are big fans of Bluehost and use a Genesis Framework and Theme on our WordPress websites.

You can get further help with building your website by visiting DanMoskelUniversity.com, and our YouTube channel ... you can also grab a copy of our book "How To Create a Website Easy Button" for a detailed step by step guide to creating a website, just like mine.

On a side note, you can use affiliate marketing offline. You can send direct mail, like Bluehost did in the earlier example, and use offline advertising. We will discuss this in more details later.

Chapter 6 - Market Research ... Go To The MONEY

The third step is for you to go find and work within competitive markets. If there is a lot of competition, that means there is a lot of money.

If there is no competition, it is a good chance there is no money. Let's take this one step further, because if you have a lot of competition within a specific market, then you can assume you will have a lot of companies that you can work with, as an affiliate to market their products and services.

Useful Tools

Please, go and do some market research using some reliable tools. One such tool, is the Google keyword planner, you can access this through the Google AdWords interface.

It will provide you with search data that you can use to determine what exactly people are typing into the search engines. This is also called a keyword tool.

For example, if your writing a page about "credit repair" when you use the Google keyword planner, you can see exactly how often that specific search term is typed into Google on a monthly basis, with this example it is approximately 33,000 times, every single month!

This will also give you related search terms and their volume. For example the keyword term "credit repair companies" is searched in Google roughly 5,400 times a month, "credit repair reviews" about 700 times a month, and "credit score repair" 590 times per month.

Some of the other related keyword terms include:

- Fast credit repair
- Free credit repair
- Credit repair companies
- Credit repair credit cards
- Credit repair after bankruptcy
- Credit repair help
- Free credit report
- How to rebuild credit
- How to fix your credit
- How to improve credit score
- Clean up credit

- Get credit score
- How to raise your credit score
- And many more

These related search terms are good subjects for additional webpages, YouTube videos, marketing materials, etc.

Remember, the Google keyword planner is just looking at Google searches. The search volume does not include Yahoo, and Bing. You can assume their is more search traffic across all three of the big search engines, along with very similar search keyword terms. In other words, it is safe to apply this information to Yahoo and Bing.

Still choosing your niche?

If your having difficulty choosing a niche consider these questions to help:

- What products or services have you recently bought and used?

- What is a recent travel experience you've had?

- What are your hobbies?

- What do you do in your free time?

And if you still can't choose or want to work within a proven lucrative market, I would suggest sub prime credit, just like I did when I got started.

It is important to have knowledge already, but just like with our kids going through school, you will continue to learn new things as your experience grows.

This is progress and just the way the world works ... it is a good thing. And something I'm most grateful for.

And follow the Napolean Hill quote:

> "If you are not sure which way to move, it is better to shut your eyes and move in the dark than to remain still and make no move at all."

Blueprint Summary & Check Up

At this point, you should be working on the first 3 steps in your blueprint:

1. Choosing your subject material

2. Building a website

3. Doing some ESSENTIAL market research

4. Creating, planning, and working on information to share about your subject and related keyword terms

Get busy now, and take action this instant ... if you can't PLEASE, grab a piece of paper and start jotting your thoughts, notes, and plans down on paper!

Don't over-think and stay relaxed.

And get busy planning and doing!

Use the Google keyword planner, it will return again and I use it almost daily. It is a VERY useful tool ... you currently have to create a Google AdWords account, which may authorize your credit card for a nominal fee such as $5.00 ... but even if you don't use your AdWords account, for anything other than this keyword tool ... it is worth it!

Next, let's talk about GETTING PAID!
And, don't forget to visit DanMoskelUniversity.com and sign up for a free bonus affiliate marketing training videos.

Chapter 7 - Getting Paid ... Affiliate Networks

The fourth step is to apply to work with an affiliate network. This is the company that is going to pay you, and actually write you a check.

Their job is to go and negotiate with advertisers and businesses looking for additional traffic.

Then, they provide you with an easy-to-use interface to access marketing materials such as website banners. In order to drive additional traffic to these businesses and advertisers.

The network is the bridge between you and the business you are marketing.

We would suggest, that you start with the 'big boys' in the industry that have an established track record. This can help you avoid working with any of the less reputable networks.

Some of the companies we suggest and have worked with include:

- Commission Junction (CJ)
- Clickbooth
- Amazon Associates Program
- Share-a-sale
- And many, many, many, more

At one point in time, Google, even had an affiliate network.

You can also find niche affiliate networks, for example within the financial niche, you could work with the Bankrate.com affiliate program.

Your Other Option ... Work Direct with the Advertiser

If you can, some of the bigger companies with affiliate marketing programs, may offer a direct relationship to work with you. This means they have an in-house network.

From our experience this provides you with a much more lucrative payout. In other words, you can create a relationship that will put more money in your pocket for the exact same traffic.

This eliminates the third party affiliate network. The third party network often takes a cut of your payout, and this way you can avoid that extra mouth to feed, and chances are earn higher revenue by working directly with the advertiser.

The Application Process

You typically will need to apply to work with networks and advertisers. You will then again need to apply for specific advertisers within different affiliate networks. Unless, you work directly with an advertiser.

You will apply as a publisher, and this commonly requires a website URL address, the amount of your monthly website traffic, plans to promote affiliate offers, and your personal information.

Your application will then be reviewed and you may get a phone call from the network, just to check in with you.

If you have any difficulty in this process, reach out and pick up the phone, write an email, and tell them your new and just getting started.

Most networks will be happy to provide you some tips and get you approved. As an FYI, this can happen with specific advertisers too.

Choosing Your Offer ... Leads or Sales

Did you know, you can generate revenue just by providing lead information for some companies.

One company we have worked with provides a $5 payout if someone submits a phone number, email address, and the best time to call for a free consultation. It doesn't matter if this lead results in a sale or not, we get paid just for a lead.

Generally speaking, we have found creating sales to be more lucrative than leads. However, you should test some different offers to find out what works best for you and your niche market.

Timetable on Your Commission Paycheck

When you earn money with affiliate marketing, you will often get paid on a monthly basis. For example, Commission Junction will issue a payment around February 16th for our earnings for the month of January.

Some networks can make you wait longer, but you can occasionally negotiate for faster payouts.

For instance, with one sub prime credit card I was marketing, due to the amount of volume and in part to using pay-per-click advertising, it was mutually beneficial for the advertiser to send us a paycheck, every other week.

This way we could continue advertising, and help growing both of our businesses together. Remember, your on the same team with the network and advertiser. You want to help each other both produce more and earn more money.

Technology

Some direct advertisers and specifically Commission Junction an affiliate network, we work with, will provide you a unique toll-free phone number for you to use with your marketing materials.

This toll-free phone number is very helpful in promoting and marketing certain products and services. It will track and credit your account with the sales made over the phone using your unique toll-free phone number.

This does not require any online activity. But we do of course enthusiastically encourage you to use in all of your marketing materials, including online.

When this technology first emerged, it produced a significant increase in conversions with a professional credit repair law firm, we were working with. It literally brought in thousands of extra dollars that was previously lost.

If you can access a toll-free phone number I definitely encourage you too, just make sure it is a number that will track your sales. Generally speaking, a toll-free phone number helps converting higher priced items and services.

Good Affiliate Networks and Managers

The good affiliate networks and managers, will want to work with you. They will want to help you, so you can help them and both build your businesses.

Your manager is the contact person you will have at the network. The good ones will communicate often with you, provide you information on hot offers, new product features, and overall useful information to help you.

Remember, you have a mutually beneficial relationship with your affiliate network. The better you do, they better they do.

We have gotten early notices for advertisers upcoming media campaigns, product launches, and features that we were able to leverage into some easy revenue.

One such example includes in the early days of my career. A manager shared with me about a new diet supplement that was going to roll out a big TV campaign.

I created a website and mopped up with revenue using SEO (free, natural, organic) search traffic, and pay-per-click advertising ...

The TV campaign created massive search traffic and there was NO competition because no one else knew about this new product. This is just one small example of what a good manager can do to help you!

Leverage for higher payouts

You must be producing in order to start leveraging your performance. If you've got some reliable volume with good traffic, we would encourage you to start asking.

You can simply ask for a raise. It will be essential for you to share with your partners how they benefit by increasing your payout.

It helps if you can point to your past performance, and also share your plans to grow your numbers with the affiliate offer through a higher payout.

For example, a higher payout can give you the ability to target additional pay-per-click markets, test some new traffic sources, etc. Just, make sure THEY see the benefit to giving you more money.

This is especially true, working directly with advertisers. We have created incentive driven payout contracts. In other words, we had a contract that would pay us more money if we could produce more sales, per month.

For example:

If you do 20 transactions in a month then you get paid $10 per transaction. If however you are able to do 50 transactions in a month, then you get paid $20 per transaction.

These numbers are merely an example, the point is the more volume you can produce from good traffic, the better and the higher a payout you should be receiving.

It makes common sense, you are providing essential value in sales for a company and/or network for an advertiser.

Shop For the Highest Bidder

One of the best ways we have received higher payouts is by attending marketing conferences and specifically Affiliate Summit.

This gives you the ability to put in valuable face time with your manager, and speak in person with the companies your working with.

You can also shop your offers with other networks to find the best payout. You can talk with a number of different networks, share with them your production, and ask what they are willing to pay you for your performance.

This is a very effective strategy to give yourself a raise. Frequently, networks will bid against one another to attract 'super affiliates'.

This is because the network has your traffic and other 'super affiliates' traffic to offer an advertiser.

One Affiliate Summit conference in Las Vegas provided us the opportunity to plant the seed for a new contract with one of our biggest partners. When we returned, we followed up with our manger by sending a performance or incentive based contract proposal over.

If I remember correctly, we went from a $17 payout to a $30 payout ... which we hit almost instantly ...

This was all EXTRA money to our bottom line, and enabled us to increase our performance for this advertiser. Just so you know, this was working directly with an advertiser, and not through a third party network.

The contract went something like this:

- 500 or less equal $17 payout
- 600 to 700 equal $18 payout
- 700 to 800 equal $19 payout
- 800 to 900 equal $20 payout
- 900 to 1000 equal $21 payout
- Etc.

You can see how an extra $5 increase to our payout, when you have a monthly volume of 1,000 actions, will result in an extra $5,000 of revenue, per month. Or $60,000 per year!

The idea is simply, the more business you can create, the more money an advertiser or network will pay you. It is just like the job position of a salesman, when you can create sales and business you are one of the most valuable assets, to any company your working with.

As you are able to negotiate higher payouts, additional traffic avenues will open up such as pay-per-click advertising. We were able to negotiate a high enough payout that it was worth it for us to pay upwards of $2 for one single click with paid advertising!

Using paid advertising can ensure the volume of your traffic, along with supplement your earnings with SEO traffic, video marketing traffic, email marketing, and more.

Just like with everything it does take time, but you can assume that every initial payout listing is much lower than what you can ultimately achieve with it.

This means, you can usually negotiate to get more money out of every affiliate marketing offer. With the earlier example, as of the writing of this book, that offer is listed with a $4 payout. But, they were paying us 6 to 7 times that as a payout!

Another company we worked with, is listed in networks at a $45 payout but if you work directly with that advertiser they will start your payout at $65. This specific advertiser negotiated to pay us a $90 payout.

Reliable volume with good traffic will put you in the drivers seat of your affiliate marketing business. You can negotiate with different companies, different affiliate networks, different offers and I would encourage you to, in order to help you find the best routes for maximum profitability, which is every business owners number #1 obligation.

Chapter 8 - Easiest Way to Get Started

The fifth step is to get started, one of the best and easiest ways to get started with affiliate marketing, is to create a website reviewing products and services, you have purchased and used.

One example is, to simply write a review about a specific product or service you have used. You can write book reviews, product reviews, video game reviews, and much more.

One way I use this strategy, is to create credit card reviews for my websites. These reviews go through the fine print and legal jargon of the terms and service, and translate that into understandable english, so people really know how a credit card actually works.

We include the benefits, the application process, features, fees, drawbacks, our experience with the credit card, and what we think about it overall.

We've used this strategy for advertisers we work with as an affiliate, along with advertisers we don't work with.

Warning

We do want to caution you and inform you, that you can get some legal backlash from this approach. Let me share, an example from my business.

When the prepaid debit card market first emerged there were a few less than ethical companies working within this niche.

One such company would charge cardholders $1 for every single transaction, the cardholder made using the card, during a calendar month!

Then, the cardholder would have to wait an additional calendar month before getting a refund for the excess $1 fees that were above the $10 monthly fee.

For folks, like myself and my spending habits, these cardholders could potentially make 100 transactions in a month and have to wait over 30 days to be refunded the extra $90 in fees, the company issuing this card withdrew from the cardholder's account.

Not too many individuals would be happy about this or are in a financial position where they can have $90 in excess fees, just held for 30 days, 60 days, or any excessive period of time.

It is ludicrous! This was a celebrity endorsed prepaid card and they sent me dozens of cease-and-desist letters. These letters threatened lawsuits, over and over again.

I corresponded with this company a number of times and did revise and update my review, once they stopped using this deceptive tactic.

I was even willing to work with them as an affiliate, but once the legal eagles get involved whose income is derived from the advertiser, they typically make empty threats and demand unreasonable things, from my experience.

Lawyers ...

If a company has a legitimate claim then comply, but if they are making threats and being deceptive which has been the majority of my experience, then you choose what path you decide is best.

At one juncture, during the years of cease-and-desist letters from this company I told them to go ahead and sue me.

You know what happened?

Nothing. Eventually, they went away only to reemerge again a few years later but again went away.

(* This is not legal advice, seek out a professional if you need help.)

The point and moral of all this, is you can really help people avoid some bad products and services. And help them find good ones, the products and services you recommend to your friends and family.

This one specific webpage created thousands of dollars, if not tens of thousands of dollars, and potentially hundreds of thousands of dollars in revenue for my business, over the years through SEO and pay-per-click traffic.

This was in large part due to the celebrity endorsement and HUGE media TV campaigns for the prepaid debit card.

For many years, my website review of this sucky prepaid card was listed directly below their website in the search engines. On our webpage we suggested that you get a competing prepaid debit card with a much more fee friendly structure.

Chapter 9 - Related Products and Services

The sixth step is to look into related products and services for your niche market that you can potentially work with. The reason for this is because your website visitor has many related interests, and you can market additional products and services to them.

Let's just look at a website visitor in the sub prime credit niche, as an example. These folks could be interested in:

- Professional credit repair service

- Bankruptcy information

- Debt consolidation

- Credit monitoring services

- Prepaid debit card

- Secured credit card

- Bank account / checking account

- Tax help

- And many more products and services

You may want to experiment with affiliate marketing and offering products and services on your website, that have mass or broad appeal. For example, you could try:

- Travel websites
  (Travelocity, Orbitz, Expedia)

- Online dating websites
  (Match.com, eHarmony)

In addition, Amazon offers an affiliate marketing program where you can sell books, electronics, hardware tools, kitchen appliances, and much more.

Your primary goal when it comes to affiliate marketing is to create an information business. In other words, you want to create a following and herd of people that are interested in you and want your subject material.

This requires you to be knowledgeable about your subject. Along with honesty, transparency, integrity, and being ethical. Be a friend to the folks that sign up to be on your list and you'll be able to create a long lasting and profitable relationship with them, and really help.

Chapter 10 - Make Money Online ... NOW

The seventh step is do it now. You must get good and busy creating useful, knowledgeable, and helpful information. This will keep you in control of your business. And put you in the drivers seat to choose which companies you want to market.

The other key tip to remember is affiliate marketing is only one of many ways to earn money online!

We strongly encourage you to experiment with Google AdSense or other advertising platforms, you can create your own products, services, and even write a book and sell that!

We will show you how to write your very own book, and to check out the process we went through creating this book just visit Dan Moskel's YouTube channel page.

Stay motivated and remember the saying:

"Ideas are worthless, unless we act on them."

So, get busy, and start harvesting your acres of diamonds, by acting on YOUR ideas!

Blueprint Summary & Check In

At this point you should be working on:

1. Applying to affiliate networks ... or advertisers directly

2. Building your website and adding new keyword related webpages

* If your feeling "stuck" review recent books you've read, products you've purchased, locations you've visited, services you've used. ... DO ANYTHING ... :)

And don't forget to visit DanMoskelUniversity.com and sign up for our free bonus affiliate marketing training videos

Section 3 - The 7 Best, Proven, Ways To Drive Traffic To Your Website Including Quick, Easy, And Free Methods

Chapter 11 - The 7 Best & Proven Traffic Sources Overview

You must have people to communicate with and send your marketing messages to, in order to earn any money with affiliate marketing.

In this section, we are going to cover the 7 best traffic sources.

These are the primary ways I drive and have always driven traffic to my websites, marketing information, and used to help serve people. The more traffic you have, the better!

Let's go ahead and list these 7 traffic sources and get busy discussing them.

1. SEO (Search Engine Optimization)

This is the natural, free, organic search result listings. This traffic is some of the best, and once you obtain high rankings with traffic on keywords ... you rarely lose that traffic ... In other words, it has the potential to last forever!

2. Email Marketing

It is vital that you view your business, as a real legit information business. You can swap out affiliate products and services, the real value is being able to access and receive your information.

An integral part of this is collecting your website visitors contact information like an email address and continuing to follow up with them. By sending them information of value and real help, you will build a relationship with the people on your list. And you will create a following for yourself and your business.

3. YouTube Videos

This is an EXCELLENT way to create, nourish, and build the relationship you have with your fans and followers. In addition to growing your business.

We have used it to help grow all 3 of our businesses, and strongly encourage you to use it too. You can also earn money using Google AdSense from your YouTube videos. Plus, you can even drive traffic to your website with your videos, details coming up.

4. Pay-Per-Click Advertising (paid advertising)

This is creating an advertisement for Google, Bing, Yahoo to display along side keyword search results. This is some of the best traffic and also some of the most expensive ... but for us it was worth spending huge sums of money for! These advertisements show up in yellow and on the right side of search result pages.

5. Content Advertising (banner ads on other websites ... paid advertising)

There are a number of ways to do this but we recommend using Google AdWords, this is the "content network" ... it will show your advertisement on other related websites.

For example, you could have your website advertisement show up on my website if we were talking about similar subject material. If your familiar, this is advertising and showing up within the Google AdSense platform. AdSense is a way I can display your paid advertisement on my website.

We have found some traffic sources in the content network are pure GOLD, and will provide dirt cheap conversions with great traffic. And others are NOT.

6. Social Media and Other People

This of course is Twitter, Facebook, Google+ and more. The simple explanation is to go where the people are, already.

Along, with reaching out to leaders in your industry and asking for help, and how best to be successful with this.

7. Offline Tactics

Yup, there are offline affiliate marketers. These folks I've seen create direct relationships with other businesses, and use direct marketing like a postcard mailing with the first example and the Bluehost web hosting company promoting the Google AdWords service.

Don't forget ... track your website traffic and conversions

There are some easy ways to track your website traffic and conversions. I want to keep this as simple as possible, and not overwhelm you, just make sure to have some tracking tools in place.

I use Google Webmaster Tools, along with StatCounter. Both these services are free, and will provide you information about your website traffic, including keyword search terms, traffic sources to your website like (YouTube) and the behavior of visitors once, they land on your website.

Track your affiliate marketing conversions

You can do this within your affiliate network interface, where you will access the marketing materials. This is often called a 'tid' or 'sub-tid' and will enable you to see what pages on your website and placements are creating sales.

You can also have a tracking code placed by the network if your using online paid advertising. This is a very easy process, we have done it dozens of times.

The online advertising platform will provide you a code that you can forward to your contact person or manager at the network and ask them to place it for you.

This code will go on the advertisers 'thank you' page ... this way you can track and see EXACTLY how much money you pay for a new customer and it will exponentially make it easier for you to cut out the wasteful spending on bad keyword terms, and crummy content websites.

This tracking is monumental in helping to capitalize on the surprise diamond keyword markets, that seem to exist in every industry.

You can find some more information along with the process of placing tracking codes by visiting DanMoskelUniversity.com and our YouTube channel.

Chapter 12 - SEO, Search Engine Optimization, Free, Natural, Organic Search Traffic

First, things first. When talking about SEO or search engine optimization we are thinking equity, not simply income. This is an investment of your time and resources instead of money.

SEO is worth the investment! And a great source of traffic!

It won't happen overnight, but this is truly one of the best, and most effective, and efficient ways to earn recurring money online! It is a full subject in and of itself.

This is why we will recommend you grab a copy of our book "SEO Training Manual - The 10 Golden Steps To Shower In Search Engine Traffic" ... and visit our website to attend one of our free Google+ Hangout SEO Training Events.

Search engine optimization is the free natural and organic search engine results.

We would encourage you to plan on using SEO which has changed dramatically over the years. Today, it will require you to first put in the wood or the work before you can get the heat and the income.

It also requires you to work smart. You must use a keyword tool such as the Google keyword planner, like we do. This helps you to create precise targets for new website pages, and YouTube videos you create.

It gives you a clearly defined goal to work towards. And eliminates foolishly throwing darts at a dart board, with your eyes closed.

If you don't use a keyword tool, you may be targeting a keyword term that is searched for only 50 times a month, when instead you could target a keyword term that is searched for 1,000 times a month.

Bite-size objectives

As we mentioned, we work in the credit niche and to get a website to rank on the keyword search term "credit repair" one of the most competitive keyword terms.

We would have to spend I'm estimating $5 per click with pay-per-click advertising, but with SEO to get our website ranked for this competitive keyword term, we are competing with dozens of other websites that have been doing SEO for that keyword term, for over a decade.

In other words, instead go scoop up the easy, lucrative, keyword markets and set your secondary target as your big picture goals with the more competitive keyword terms.

You can get ranked for any keyword term but, think in terms of return on investment. Let's first get some recurring income and the easy money, while we work toward the big money.

If you choose to go into the sub prime credit niche for example, you have to have realistic goals when you're starting out.

I would encourage you to aim for less competitive and related keyword markets.

Using the example of "credit repair" some related search keyword markets, that would be better and easier to start with include:

- Legal credit repair

- How to build credit

- How to remove bad credit

- Credit cards for bad credit

- Clean up credit report

- Raise credit score

- Get credit score

- And many more.

A rule of thumb I follow is to look for a minimum of roughly 100 searches per month, with the keyword tool, anything with more than 100 monthly searches is a keyword term I will pursue.

It is very helpful, if you can invest some money with pay-per-click advertising. This will help you to discover which keyword search terms convert into sales and commission earnings for you, inside of a new niche.

This can by very helpful to focusing your SEO efforts on proven keyword converting terms.

If you are not earning money with paid advertising, obviously STOP! But, take full advantage and make use of the information you collect on the converting keyword terms!

The basics to SEO

1. Title Tag

The title of your webpage should use the keyword search term you want that page to show up for. This is what shows up in blue for your website in search result pages.

2. Meta description

The meta description, is the two sentence summary about what your webpage contains. You also see this in the search result pages.

3. Content and more

Your webpage content, how useful it is, how credible the author is, how big your website is, and many more factors.

If you start with doing good keyword research, choosing good titles, using a good description, and writing useful content your off to an AMAZING start.

I encourage you to check out the Google SEO Starter Guide for a more comprehensive review of the basics.

One of the biggest mistakes is to not take a moment and use a keyword tool.

I recommend using the Google keyword planner. This will show you what exact terms are searched and approximately how often. This way you can title your webpages using the high search keyword terms and targeting rankings for keyword terms you know get lots of traffic.

It will also help you avoid targeting keyword terms that get minimal traffic or worse yet no traffic. It doesn't mean much, and won't earn you any money if your ranked #1 for a keyword term, if it is NOT being searched for and providing traffic to your website.

Creating webpages about related high volume search terms will also help your SEO. This traffic source is similar to a snowball rolling down a hill. It picks up momentum and gathers speed and MORE traffic.

The initial investment is the most difficult part, however I am currently still earning money from information I wrote YEARS ago! You can do this too!

Chapter 13 - Strategy ... Target Buying Keywords

One of the easier places to start with is reviews of other big businesses products and services. These can be products you've recently purchased, currently use, or are knowledgeable about.

The idea is, that this particular business will generate search traffic. I used the earlier examples of products being advertised on TV creating massive search traffic, this is a great strategy to follow!

For example, if you were writing about the "American Express Credit Card" you can assume there is substantial search traffic because American Express is a household name.

Let me say again, it's very smart to use the Google keyword planner and get specifics about the keyword search volume.

With this example the keyword term "American Express Credit Card" (singular) is searched almost 15,000 times a month.

Compare that to the "American Express Credit Cards" (plural) which is only searched roughly 2,400 times a month.

This means you should target the singular keyword term and title your review page something like:

"American Express Credit Card - Review of How It Works"

For the advanced user, you could also include in your meta description something about the "American Express Credit Card Application" because that is also an indicator the search engines use, when ranking your website.

It will tell the search engines you are relevant to the keyword search term "American Express Credit Card Application" which is searched for about 700 times every month.

We can assume many of those searches are made by people wanting to apply for the credit card. In other words, it's a buying keyword search term instead of an informational search.

If search engine optimization is foreign to you, the search engines are getting very sophisticated and will assume your site is about singular and plural versions along with related keywords ... but your objective is to create your website and webpages, highlighting the biggest volume search terms (or your target phrase).

Heads up

Frequently, you will not be able to use pay-per-click advertising on "trademark" terms for a company you are working with. With the above example we are using the "American Express" trademark term.

You can target the SEO listings, without any problems but with paid advertising if you advertise on their trademarked terms you are usually increasing their advertising expenses.

In other words, you're competing with them. In any business with any sense, they will only allow their top super affiliates to advertise on their trademark keyword terms.

This can potentially include you but not out of the gates and not immediately. That is only with pay-per-click advertising.
Example:

If you were affiliate marketing with an offer like "Nike shoes" chances are you would not be permitted to use paid advertising on the keyword term "Nike shoes."

There is typically less competition with both paid and SEO traffic on a specific business or product. Using the above example if you are to target "Nike shoes" ... you would have much less competition than targeting the keyword terms:

- Shoes
- Men's shoes
- Athletic shoes
- Running shoes
- Etc.

We recommend you target these more general terms, but also target terms like Nike shoes, Adidas shoes, Reebok shoes, Converse shoes, and other competing shoe companies.

As we mentioned the companies that pay you, rarely want you to use paid advertising on their trademark terms.

We have discovered SEO and pay-per-click traffic for similar products keyword terms can be very effective, often times cheap, and good converting sources of traffic to sales.

If you're working with a company marketing their products and services. It is vitally important that you follow their rules, such as not advertising on their trademarked terms if that is one of their requirements.

If you neglect to follow a networks rules or an advertisers requirements, that network and or advertiser can stop working with you. This can be a very expensive path, I've personally dealt with it and don't recommend it.

Most advertisers will have a few specific guidelines that you need to follow and possibly some traffic sources that they do not want and traffic they do want.

Why is this?

This is for a few reasons one of which is the advertisers pay-per-click advertising budget.

Another reason is because of fraud with affiliate marketing.

There was one small company we spoke with at an Affiliate Summit conference who told us they had listed their product as an advertiser to get additional traffic, but the majority of the traffic they received was fraudulent.

In other words, they paid tens of thousands of dollars for nothing! If your considering putting your business as an advertiser on an affiliate network, use some caution.

Related industries

One of the better ways we have been able to achieve good search traffic is on related keyword terms. Specifically within the credit niche there is massive search traffic for different collection agencies names.

For example:

You get a letter in the mail from a company you have never heard of, claiming you owe them $300.

Your first reaction is to probably search the name of this company that you have never done business with, and then you can potentially land on one of my websites that talks about how you can fight this alleged debt, settle it, and how to deal with this specific collection agency ... there are 100's of collection agencies, and this is just one example, but use your imagination there are related markets for you to target with SEO and paid advertising in every industry.

Non-converting webpages

It is important to focus your SEO efforts on proven keywords that you know will convert into affiliate sales and commissions for you.

We have discovered within every niche there are some keyword terms that just don't convert very well. These non-converting keyword terms just don't convert well with anything. They are more informational driven searches.

One such example within the credit niche is:

- "do it yourself credit repair"
- "credit repair letters"
- "credit report dispute letter"

And a variety of other terms. Many of these folks are typically looking for just information like, how-to advice, and templates for a dispute letter because they are fixing their credit themselves.

For niche webpages that you just can't seem to find an affiliate offer that will convert on it, please try Google AdSense or another advertising network, so you can host advertisements instead.

This is a great way to monetize your website traffic on those keyword terms. We like Google

AdSense but there are a number of other companies you can work with too.

These companies will provide you a code just like affiliate marketing and you simply copy and paste that code into your website. You can see a video of this on my YouTube channel.

It is a genius idea for any and every new business to spend a little bit of money to do appropriate research into their target market before you invest huge time into SEO.

This way you can discover what keywords really drive sales and what keywords do not.

I am confident, you will be pleasantly surprised by some smaller low cost paid advertising slices of the market. Once you find some of these, then focus your SEO efforts on those exact keyword terms.

These traffic sources, can be very lucrative income streams with both paid and natural organic SEO traffic. Invest your time, and energy and even shoestring advertising budget on the optimal places to help grow your business fast, and then you can expand into the more competitive markets, along with negotiating higher affiliate payouts.

Chapter 14 - Email Marketing

You will get the most benefit if you start building a list and follow up with people using email marketing. This will also give you the opportunity to provide more service, and help people with your information. This will help build your brand, trust, goodwill and opportunities to earn more money with affiliate marketing.

Building your list

One effective way to build your list is to create a web-form offering a free report. Visitors to your website can sign up and will be automatically emailed your free report.

Then you can continue to follow up with these folks. You don't have to send them to affiliate marketing offers either, you can send them messages to check out your YouTube videos, new pages on your website, and use affiliate marketing.

This list of people is BIG EQUITY you have with your business! The better a relationship you have with your list, the more income you will earn from it.

Shoestring budget

If you have a shoestring budget you can create a free account at MailChimp to collect your website visitors email address. You can also send a limited number of marketing messages, but this is all free. If your funds are tight, we recommend using MailChimp to start.

We personally use Aweber, they give you the first month for $1, then $19.99 per month for 500 subscribers. We like the additional features and options Aweber provides us, with special attention to the ability to split test web-forms on our website.

Some web-forms convert much better than others ... with a free MailChimp account you do not get these extra features we like so much ...

You can always move your list of leads to any email marketing service you choose, at any point in time!

* Please, turn off a confirmation message. This is the email that asks people "if they really want

your information..." this option DESTROYS your conversion rate and is like trying to sell something twice. Once you get a "yes" ... shut your mouth and give them what they want!

Follow up

You should create some follow up campaigns to send your list. You want to build a relationship and you want to earn additional money. If your information is good, then people will consume it, assuming you use enough marketing insights to get their attention and your email messages opened.

Email marketing is a marketing tool to help build every business and can provide you with an automatic income funnel using affiliate marketing! It's great to be able to set up campaigns and let them run on autopilot!

However, many businesses aren't doing this, at least not very well yet. Which is why we've seen a great response to our most recent book "Email Marketing That Works ... So You Don't Have To"

We are going to hold a Google + Hangouts Email Marketing Training Event we suggest you sign up to attend along with checking out our YouTube channel ... we are sincere in our desire to HELP you!

Feel free to reach out to us too! We would love to hear from you and hope to help you overcome any current marketing challenges you are facing!

4 Tips to Success

We will quickly give you a run down of our basics to success with email marketing and what we have found.

1. Test your web-forms ... different colors, headlines, giveaways

As we mentioned, different web forms convert at different rates ... work to find the best web-form and always be split testing your web-forms.

It also helps to send shorter email marketing messages to drive traffic to read an article on your website, watch your YouTube video, then from there use affiliate marketing, but send useful helpful information. And avoid trying to make a sale in your email message.

2. Send videos

Sending, YouTube videos in your email messages seem to get a great click thru. As in people like to go watch a short YouTube video you create.

3. Direct marketing

Use direct marketing tactics and strategies. This means you must get your lists attention, and time so you can market an offer to them. We strongly, encourage you to look into some additional resources such as Dan Kennedy and one of his great books "The Ultimate Sales Letter."

4. Ask questions and provide help

Ask if you can help people on your list. Often, you will have folks reach out to you, asking you for help. When this happens ... HELP THEM!

Once, you help them share your interaction with other people on your list. One person's challenge and question is also another persons. And that other person is likely on your list.

Just by helping the people on your list you are serving them. And as Earl Nightingale says:

"The amount of service you provide others, is in direct proportion to the amount of income you earn."

Chapter 15 - YouTube Videos

Many companies, including myself use YouTube videos to drive traffic and share helpful information. We've also seen some folks use affiliate marketing directly from their YouTube videos.

We encourage you to first check out the full YouTube Terms of Service to make sure you are compliant.

YouTube is a great way of sharing your message, growing your list, and your business.

It is also smart to apply some SEO basics to your YouTube videos. We have seen these YouTube watch pages do EXTREMELY well in the search engine results.

In other words, your YouTube video can get ranked and get traffic from the search engine keyword results, just like your website. We use SEO on almost every video we create, we use it in the title, our video description, and tags. The tags are your actual keyword targets.

Video Marketing Tips

The key to using video marketing is to create engaging, helpful, and useful information in your videos. You can and will build a following of people that like you and want to see your latest stuff.

If your already using Google AdSense, you can also earn money from your videos. This is very easy to do, once you associate your AdSense account, you can simply check a box and have advertisements show up on your videos. There are some additional features you can use with advertisements.

We use YouTube to drive traffic to our website and collect visitors contact information. Along with using affiliate marketing and selling our books through Amazon and their Associates Program.

The Amazon Associates Program is an affiliate marketing program. I believe they choose "associates" because it sounds better. But they will provide you the ability to sell products and services on your website through Amazon.

You can find videos with more details about working as an Amazon partner on Dan Moskel's YouTube channel.

Call to Action

In many of our YouTube videos, our call to action is to visit our website and "grab your free copy of the 7 super simple steps to clean your credit."

We strongly suggest you comply with the exact YouTube terms and conditions. This is an effective way to share your message, knowledge, and create leads along with visitors to your website very quickly.

You can easily schedule a campaign of follow up emails to be sent along with your free report.

Through these follow up methods and our free report we use affiliate marketing, along with sending folks directly to our website, and YouTube videos that are also monetized with AdSense.

Use everything that you discover to be a viable income stream to earn money online! Only focus on the best and most effective ways that you find for your niche.

The big variety we have seen is from one niche subject to another such as credit information ... and dating information. This is one reason, you should work inside competitive markets because it is likely there will be a lot of ways to generate revenue.

You can put videos on your website, and we encourage you to build some text links from your website to your videos, and share your videos on social media sites.

If you have good, useful information to share with people, you will start building a following on YouTube, which can translate into website visitors, members on your list, customers, clients, and revenue for your business.

The MOST important factor to your success is your desire to REALLY help other people!

You have a wealth of knowledge and the more you can share with others and serve other people, the more income you will earn!

Chapter 16 - Pay-Per-Click Advertising

This is paid advertising and a way you can buy instant traffic to your website. You will choose keyword terms that your website is about.

For example, you could say I want my advertisement to display every time someone searches "how to talk to women" and I'm willing to pay $.65 per click.

Then, when someone searches this term in Google, Yahoo, and Bing my advertisement will show up. I only pay if the advertisement is actually clicked on by the searcher. You will need to use Google AdWords and Bing Ads to move forward with pay-per-click.

This traffic source, is a great tool that can give you instant feedback and useful insights into your niche market. And often, we have been surprised by some very profitable traffic avenues.

You have complete control, and can advertise even on a shoestring budget. You can set daily spend limits, geographic or regional targeting, and many more sophisticated options.

One huge benefit to pay-per-click advertising is once you find and get some things working and profitable, this traffic source is instantly scalable.

One of the most effective strategies for my business is to use paid advertising to provide insights into our SEO work and high converting keyword search terms.

For example:

One keyword term includes "credit repair services" and "credit repair companies." If you are using affiliate marketing for a professional credit repair attorney, these keyword search terms are exponentially more profitable than some of the other even more competitive keyword search markets.

It was VERY SMART and profitable for us to focus on these specific high converting keyword terms with SEO and related synonyms to "credit repair services" and "credit repair companies." Instead, of simply working to rank for the keyword term "credit repair."

Cut The Fat

It is vital that you track your website visitor traffic especially with pay-per-click advertising. Doing this will provide you the ability to optimize your campaign. You can easily cut the wasteful spending and increase spending in the profitable markets, and put the perfect sections on auto-pilot.

My Wasteful Advertising

With paid advertising on credit card keyword terms, one frequent wasted advertising keyword term is "credit card sign in" and "credit card payment" and "credit card balance" ... these specific keyword search terms, we can tell the search engines not to show our advertisement.

This can eliminate huge sums of money from your campaign budget and turn a losing ad campaign into a winning and profitable campaign.

You have to be careful with pay-per-click and use a lot of direct marketing strategies. It takes work like everything but we have found it to be worth the time, money, and investment.

This is a more cut-throat and competitive way to drive traffic to your website. By the way, I've thrown thousands of dollars away by accidentally advertising on terms like "the" "a" "card" and more ...

Unfortunately, this wasn't a one time occurrence ... you will make some mistakes too, just try to avoid making them twice ... ;)

Chapter 17 - Content Network

This is also paid advertising. The content network is how you advertise on other websites.

This can be a great source of traffic. But just like with pay-per-click advertising you must track your traffic and conversions.

You can "cut the fat" by identifying the websites with non converting traffic and maximize your earnings with the good quality websites.

Generally speaking, your advertisement here will be shown on a website about your subject material.

For example:

If you were a professional credit repair attorney, and I have a website with a page getting SEO traffic for the keyword term "credit repair attorney" ... you could advertise on my website and get traffic.

There are some good and bad sources of traffic here, you must be granular, but we have found some GOLD MINES over the years on the content network. With the example about sub prime credit cards and a $30 payout, the content network was providing us conversions on some traffic for about $5. In other words, $25 was ALL profit!

Chapter 18 - Social Media ... and Other People

Social media such as Google+, Facebook, and Twitter is where people are. Therefore you should also be there.

It will benefit your SEO on your website, along with giving your customers, clients, and fans, additional avenues to follow you.

We suggest adding a web-form to your Facebook page. Also, make regular posts with your YouTube videos, include links over to your website when you publish new pages, and anything else you want.

Ask for help

Ask the leaders in your industry for help. This can be done by providing them value and doing it first. One such way, we have plans to use this is by submitting guest articles and asking for publication with leaders in this industry.

However, when we ask them to publish our guest article, we are also going to point to places and references, along with a YouTube video that shares how much they have already helped us.

For example:

Brian Tracy, the author of over 50 books has helped me immensely. At his website they accept guest articles, and one way we are confident will increase our chances of success is by telling Brian's organization in our email asking for publication, that we have also created a testimonial YouTube video and provide the URL, along with mentioning Brian in this book and others such as "Email Marketing That Works ... So You Don't Have To."

The fact is, Brian and many business leaders in every niche want to help you. And many provide you with an affiliate program. If you have already recommend and have benefited from their information, product, or service, and have shared that with others, you are helping them and creating good will.

This will increase the chance they will help you. Our plan is to be published on Brian Tracy's website in the next 30 days, if you want to see

EXACTLY how we go about this process subscribe to Dan Moskel's YouTube channel.

You must ask ... and "ye, shall receive" ... reach out, you have nothing to lose! Make sure that you give them a good quality article that you have NOT published elsewhere, or plan to.

Other Media

If you can publish or appear in other media such as newspapers, magazines, TV ... then, it will help to establish your expertise and authority. This will also help your website SEO and organic, natural, free traffic.

One of the things human reviewers look for is your authority and if you are the author of a published book for example, you have more authority than someone who is not.

Integrity

If your suggesting to your list and fans to use products based off nothing more than your payout, you won't have a long lasting business.

People can see this come through, in your marketing messages, along with figuring out your only interested in serving your needs, instead of theirs.

If however, you do use integrity and only recommend products, services, and information that has been of benefit to you, you will establish trust with your followers, goodwill, and a mutually beneficial relationship.

Chapter 19 - Take It Offline

As we mentioned, online affiliate marketing is not the only way to use this business model. We have personally received physical mail like the postcard mentioned at the beginning of this book, along with other types of physical mail, using affiliate marketing.

In fact, what your really creating is an information marketing business. Some of the advanced teachers in this industry advise taking your leads offline.

Dave Dee recalls reading one of Dan Kennedy's sales letters, multiple times because it was a real physical letter. Just so you know, Dave Dee a former magician has now purchased and runs a big part of Dan Kennedy's business.

We have seen credit repair attorney affiliates set up a deal with car dealerships to send unqualified applicants to fix their credit, and naturally real estate agents would be an ideal fit for this too.

You may want to experiment with purchasing some more traditional offline media advertisements such as billboards, print ads, radio ads, etc. These can include a call to action to visit your website, call your unique toll-free phone number, the sky is the limit.

Traffic Summary

These 7 traffic sources are not the ONLY sources of traffic. There are tons of ways to get traffic online, and using some creativity can only benefit you!

We've recently heard of folks using Craig's List to generate very HIGH dollar transactions, along with some of the social media sites like Fiverr.com.

There is no right or wrong way to get traffic ... but of course, focus on the profitable ways ... :)

Section 4 - Advanced Tips to Make Money with Affiliate Marketing

Chapter 20 - Copywriting Tips

Your the salesman. It is key to selling, to be experienced with the item you are selling. Know, how it works, the features, the benefits, the drawbacks, everything.

I strongly encourage you to get some good resources to help with this. Such as Dan Kennedy, Perry Marshall, Ken McCarthy, and others.

A few tips include:

1. Write to just one person

Write to just one reader, or speak to just one viewer if your making a YouTube video. I like the comparison that you should be like the excited 8 year old explaining how something works.

2. Use your energy

Your level of energy will translate in your writing and speaking and every communication. Be energetic, uplifting, optimistic, and encouraging and people will be much more likely to enjoy your material and act on what you say.

3. Ask and ye shall receive

You must ask and ask multiple times for people to do what you want. If you don't ask, you will never receive.

4. Always be learning

You will get better, as long as you keep working on it. Many of the best copywriters are self-taught. It is like everything we do, and works like a muscle, the more you do the better and stronger you become.

Chapter 21 - Best Website Placement with Affiliate Marketing Banners

The very top of your website with a toll-free phone number in very easy to see locations, does great. We have also found putting a call to action in print at the end of our webpages such as:

"Call 1-800-toll-free-phone-number for a free credit consultation"

And directly below this call to action, placing an affiliate banner usually a 300x300 size, has been our best converting 'template' with affiliate marketing and any monetization methods from our websites.

Make sure you test different locations and methods, but the above tips are two big discoveries we have found.

On a side note, from my understanding placing a banner in the middle of your webpage that breaks up your article is not 'user friendly' and will not help your SEO.

Thin Affiliate Websites

One word of caution, is that the search engines have taken action against what they call "thin affiliate marketing websites" ... Check out the Google Webmaster and Matt Cuts video ... for full details. But, the short idea is you have to create good content and a website to actually help people, not just to get money.

This is one of the many reasons why you should build your website around your passion, interests, and excitement in your life. And what is most valuable to other people.

If you have website traffic, then you can earn money online ... period! If you already have website traffic I suggest trying to monetize your site with Google AdSense along with affiliate marketing and get some income generating while you test to find out what works best and where.

Do More

Whatever niche you choose, however you pursue traffic, if you do more of it, your going to get there. You may need to make some course corrections, but one key to success is by getting busy and acting!

Jim Rohn calls it the "Whiling Dervish" effect, W. Clement Stone used the "Do It Now" motto and my favorite is what Dan Kennedy calls:

"No Wonder He's So Successful Look at Everything He Does"

For more from Dan Moskel

http://www.danmoskeluniversity.com/

YouTube Channel:
http://www.youtube.com/user/dmoskel

Google+:
https://plus.google.com/+Danmoskeluniversity/posts

Facebook:
https://www.facebook.com/danmoskelpage

Please, reach out to us and let us know how your affiliate marketing efforts are coming along. I know you can do this, and do it successfully!

And don't forget to visit DanMoskelUniversity.com to sign up for your free bonus affiliate marketing training videos

Other books by Dan Moskel

1. How To Create a Website Easy Button
2. SEO Training Manual - The 10 Golden Steps to Shower In Search Engine Traffic
3. Email Marketing That Works ... So You Don't Have To

www.ingramcontent.com/pod-product-compliance
Lightning Source LLC
Chambersburg PA
CBHW051813170526
45167CB00005B/1997